THE CHANGI CROSS
A Symbol of Hope
in the Shadow of Death

By Louise Cordingly

With an introduction by Terry Waite CBE

For a detailed account of Eric Cordingly's war experiences see:

Down to Bedrock:
The Diary and Secret Notes of a Far East
Prisoner of War Chaplain 1942-45

By Eric Cordingly
Edited by Louise Cordingly

Published by Art Angels Publishing Ltd, Norwich October 2013

ISBN - 978-0-9926954-0-8

Also available on Kindle

Front cover design by Jon Bliss at MADE Agency Ltd
Design by MADE Agency Ltd
Typesetting in 12pt Bell MT

Printed in England by Swallowtail Print, Norwich, Norfolk

Published by Art Angels Publishing Ltd, Norwich

ISBN - 978-0-9926954-1-5

INTRODUCTION   by   TERRY WAITE CBE

I well remember the first time I visited Changi Museum in Singapore. I was on my way to Indonesia with a former prisoner of the Japanese, accompanying him on his return to the place where his ship was torpedoed and sunk. He had managed to swim ashore where he was immediately captured and spent the next three and a half years of his life as a prisoner. Now, sixty years later, he was returning. During our long and meaningful journey together he told me of his experiences and, like so many fellow captives, spoke of how internment brought out the best and worst in men. Always, he said, in such terrible circumstances some individuals stand out and give hope to those who find themselves in a situation that appears to be hopeless. Eric Cordingly, an Army Chaplain, was one such man. In his own quiet way he was able to engage his fellow captives in creative activity, and in many different ways help them keep hope alive.

Captives dream of freedom and reconstruct in their minds the memories of those whom they love and the places and objects that have meant so much to them in their lives. Sadly, far too many did not return to the freedom they once enjoyed. Families were left without a father and, as is recorded in this little book, many children grew up not only without knowing their father, but also not knowing how their fathers lived and died.

Having been a captive myself in very different circumstances I understand the importance of memory, but also the importance of symbols. I am writing this at a time when relationships between some professed followers of Islam and Christians are at a low ebb indeed. But in this story, in the midst of terrible deprivations, we read of a true act of generosity from one faith to another.

We also read how the Chaplain was responsible for the creation of a small brass cross for the camp chapel. Each evening prisoners gathered together around this symbol. Many years later this small object gave one man news of the father he never knew.

When I received the completed manuscript I sat down and read it through at one go. It is movingly and poignantly written and reminds all who read it that from the depths and agony of suffering, new life may be found.

August 2014

FOREWORD

In an age of throw away materialism it is difficult to imagine an existence where your worldly possessions could be carried in a kit bag. Where selling your fountain pen or trading your wedding ring may mean the difference between life and death. In a world where you could be condemned to death for stealing an egg or a gift of a tin of pineapple could save a life. Where the flame of hope is a precious commodity and can be extinguished by the slightest zephyr of ill fortune.

Our museum collection at the Changi Museum has little monetary value. Do not come to us if you wish to see gold and silver treasures; we deal in tin, wood and bamboo. Our items are functional, homemade, make do, simple items of domestic use such as cigarette cases, tooth brushes, sewing kits, tools, eating instruments. These are items that address the practicalities of day to day survival.

However we also have a collection of less functional objects such as badges, postcards, letters, photographs and trinkets. These are the trading currency of hope. The memories that are associated with these items gave their owners the strength to endure.

The Changi Cross is the quintessence of this tender. This simple item, made from scrap metal with caring hands, destined to travel into the darkest places and to adorn the altars of four POW chapels. Hundreds of men, living under the deepening shadow of death, bent their knee before this cross and in return were given strength of spirit to go on; just enough to last another day, just enough to see them through.

Today our cross trades in memories. Thousands have paused in its presence to remember the sacrifice and courage of the congregations that went before. One cross, one simple piece of metal work, is a bond to a tragic event almost beyond our understanding. As you pause before it, reach out and remember them.

This book tells of simple deeds and missing links, of common courage and fortitude beyond recall. How such a simple object forged from adversity, saved lives, bestowed hope and now keeps the memories alive.

Changi Museum and Chapel are proud to be the custodians of the Changi Cross. All proceeds from this book will be used to ensure the cross, the chapel and the museum remains as fitting tribute to those forever young who died in captivity and to the weary who survived to remember them.

And what of men like Eric Cordingly and Harry Stogden who played such a central role in the story of the Changi Cross? It is for men like these that one attends remembrance ceremonies for the fallen. These ceremonies are sometimes blamed for glorifying war. In truth there is very little that is glorious about war, for some of man's worst traits are displayed in the evil dance of human conflict; the Holocaust being a prime example.

However in the abyss of war one can also recount numerous examples of how, in the face of terrible adversity, there were men who displayed great selflessness. Their actions give hope for humanity for theirs was a nobility of spirit worthy of future generations to emulate. It is for the nobility of men like Eric Cordingly and Harry Stogden that one even celebrates remembrance ceremonies. I am grateful that future generations will get to hear their story through this book.

Jeya Ayadurai
Director
The Changi Museum

This book is dedicated to the memory of
Sergeant Harry Stogden
and
"all the other poor souls who perished"
Far East Prisoners of War 1942-45

and in loving memory of Eric and Mary Cordingly

The Changi Cross was designed, constructed and engraved by three prisoners of war in Changi, Singapore in 1942. It was taken home to the UK after the war and brought back to Changi Museum in 1992.

In the deserts of the heart

Let the healing fountain start,

In the prison of his days

Teach the free man how to praise.

W H Auden

This verse is engraved on the gravestone of
Eric and Mary Cordingly in the Jesus Chapel of Norwich Cathedral.

This is the story of a small brass cross which was forged in the horrors of war and surrender in Singapore 1942. Curiously, it has touched so many lives since its creation all those years ago, that it seems, now, to have a life of its own.

My father, Eric Cordingly, was an army chaplain during the Second World War and he was one of the 50,000 allied soldiers held prisoner by the Japanese for three and a half years in Changi, Singapore, and then 'up-country' beside the River Kwai in Thailand during the building of the notorious Death Railway. Like most of the men who came home afterwards, he rarely talked about his experiences and I've always been puzzled by his POW years. For me, tracing the history of the cross was the key to unlocking the mystery of what he called, paradoxically, 'the most wonderful time' of his life.

For an orphaned son, Bernard Stogden, who lives in Wales, the cross performed a small miracle and brought him into contact with the father he never knew. "I was only 4 years old when he went to war," he told me: "I have gone through life without a father. I missed him then and I still miss him now." Bernard and I met unexpectedly on our journeys to discover more about our fathers. This is how it all came about.

Photograph taken moments after Eric Cordingly arrived back at Leckhampton Rectory in the Cotswolds. Mary is next to him and he is holding 6 year old David's hand. 4 year old John is standing in front of Mary's grandmother, Josephine Smith. The taxi is still in the background.

In October 1946 after the war in the Far East had ended, my father came home to his wife and two small sons in Leckhampton, his parish in the Cotswolds, bringing with him just a few personal items, a brass cross and some other mementoes of the chapels he'd created when he was a prisoner of war.

He gradually recovered his health and strength and resumed his life as a parish priest. My youngest brother and I were born in the Cotswolds and completed a family of six, brought up in the benevolent atmosphere of large, draughty old rectories while the parish life went on around us. My father was a kind and gentle man with a quiet faith. The only evidence of his war years, that I noticed, were his occasional bouts of flu-like dengue fever and a liking for a pudding which was a family favourite. It was fluffy boiled rice flavoured with lashings of brown sugar, golden syrup or sweetened condensed milk. I suppose it reminded him of those days when rice had kept him alive. But my mother said that he often dreamed that he was still a prisoner. "A most frequent nightmare," he wrote, "And this does not diminish, is the feeling of being a prisoner. The loss of freedom is a terrible thing; the human spirit must be free."

In 1955 we moved to a large group parish in Stevenage and finally to Norfolk where he became Archdeacon of Norfolk and then Bishop of Thetford. Each time we moved, my father placed the brass cross on the bookshelves in his study, the room where he wrote his sermons and met with his clergy. Then, sadly, in 1976 he died of cancer aged 65, probably weakened by those terrible three and a half war years of starvation.

Eric and Mary outside the Rectory, Caistor St Edmund, near Norwich in 1970.

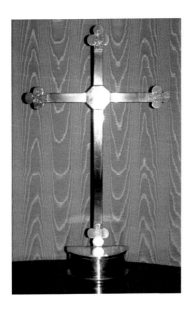

The cross remained with the Cordingly family in the UK until 1992.

My mother moved out of their rectory into a small cottage and when she was settled in she was not quite sure where to put the cross. Finally she polished it up and put it in the spare bedroom which was used by her grandchildren.

My son, James, remembers seeing it there: "It was a house full of precious things, wherever you looked, but nothing was untouchable – you were allowed to touch anything you wanted. I remember seeing the cross in the bunk room and wondering what all the markings / inscriptions meant. I knew it was important and it felt quite a privilege to have it in my bunk room."

Then in 1991 my eldest brother, David, made a trip to the Far East and when he returned he told my mother about the new Changi Prison Chapel and Museum which opened in 1988. A small open air chapel had been created to represent the chapels of all denominations constructed by the chaplains during their POW years. So my mother had the idea of sending the cross back to Singapore. My father had always intended to take her to Singapore and Thailand, but he died before they had a chance to go there. By now my mother was in her mid 70s and she was reluctant to travel so far, so my brother John and I decided to take it back for her. For the first time in my life I looked more closely at the familiar cross and realized that I knew nothing about its history.

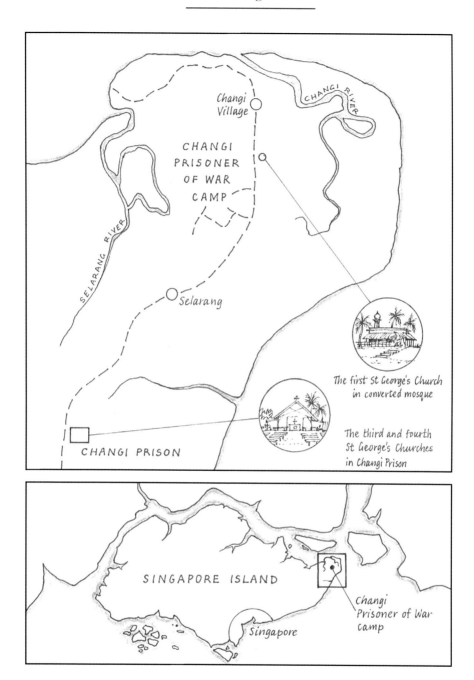

The maps show the location of Changi prisoner of war camp and Changi Prison.
St George's Mark 1 - the converted mosque, is in the POW camp and
St George's 111 and 1V are in Changi Prison.
Drawn by David Cordingly

My mother searched through her files and handed me my father's unpublished war diary: 150 thin sheets of yellowing paper tucked carefully inside a home-made cardboard cover. He had typed it up during the first year of imprisonment and had called it "Captive Christians." [the diary and his wartime notes and reports were published as "Down to Bedrock" in 2013]. There, in the typed notes, was an account of the origins and the making of the cross.

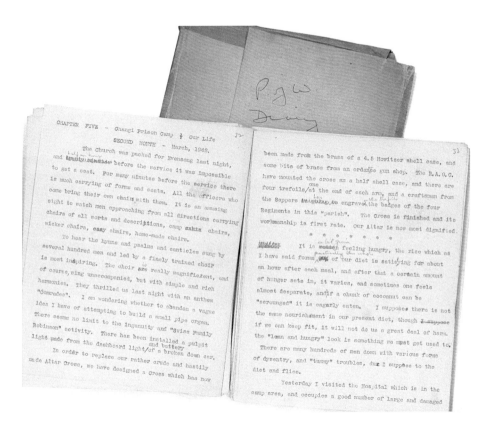

Pages from the diary Eric typed when he was in Changi 1942-43

He described the weeks of fierce fighting in Singapore, leading up to the surrender of the Allied forces on Sunday February 15th 1942. The 50,000 soldiers were ordered to surrender to the Imperial Japanese Army. They were rounded up and confined to a large disused barracks area near Changi village on the Eastern tip of Singapore.

OUTSKIRTS OF SINGAPORE Feb 42
"Fierce fighting" led up to the surrender of the Allied forces on February 15th 1942.
Painting by POW Des Bettany

As they milled about trying to settle into this new life behind the wire my father came across a small, abandoned, open-air mosque.

He wrote: "I discovered next to our billet a delightful building almost hidden by flowering shrubs and trees, purples and reds in profusion. It was a fairly large, white building with wide verandas on three sides. At one end were steps leading to a minaret upon which was a dome, and this was surmounted by the familiar Star and Crescent. ... It was obvious immediately that this little Mosque was admirably suitable for a church. ... it is both light and pleasantly cool, being open on three sides. It was not too difficult to get permission to use the building, once having this I soon had volunteers, both officers and men, who spent their first Saturday in captivity in making a Church. The results were almost miraculous."

He was very encouraged by the enthusiastic support for this new church which he called St George's (St George appears on the badge of the Royal Northumberland Fusiliers, which was his unit) and, knowing that there were several skilled craftsmen among his fellow prisoners, he took a pencil and paper and drew the design for a cross.

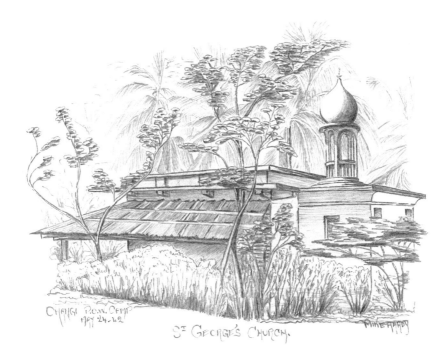

"I discovered next to our billet a delightful building almost hidden by flowering shrubs…
It was obvious immediately that this little mosque was admirably suitable for a church".
Drawing by POW Mike Hardy in Changi POW Camp May 24 1942

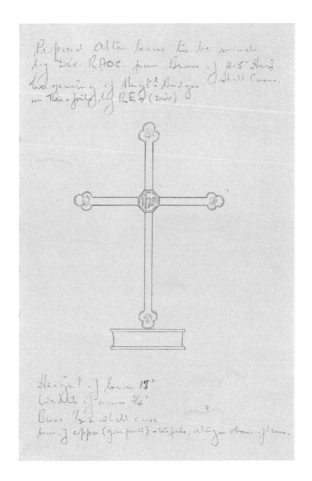

Eric's pencilled design for the new altar cross:
"to be made by Div. RAOC from brass of 4.5 howitzer shell case."

"In order to replace our rather crude and hastily made Altar Cross, we have designed a Cross which has now been made from the brass of a 4.5" howitzer shell case, and some bits of brass from an ordnance gun shop," he wrote. "The R.A.O.C (Royal Army Ordinance Corps) have mounted the cross on a half shell case, and there are four trefoils one at the end of each arm, and a craftsman from the Sappers has engraved on the trefoils the badges of the four Regiments in this "parish." The Cross is finished and its workmanship is first rate. Our Altar is now most dignified."

"The Cross is finished and its workmanship is first rate. Our Altar is now most dignified"
Pen and ink sketch by POW Payne of St George's Altar.

[The sapper, I later discovered, was Tim Hemmings of the 560th Royal Engineers, see below, page 41.] The trefoils were engraved with the badges of the four units in my father's 'parish': the RAOC, the Royal Engineers, the Royal Northumberland Fusiliers and the Royal Army Service Corps. The practice of putting a cross and candlesticks on the altar began in the 13th century and it represents the body of Christ during the celebration of mass. This is a classic Latin altar cross design (the vertical bar is longer than the horizontal) and includes the letters "IHS" which stand for the words "Jesus Christ" in Greek.

My father was a modest man but he could not help noting with pleasure the way this little church of St George's became the focus of activities in his area of Changi and gave the homesick men a sense of structure and hope. He said he had always felt a little in the way in the army but now that they had surrendered he believed that the chaplains had a wonderful opportunity: "I found there was a terrific wish for people to get back to that part of life which they knew and needed and therefore coming to church in a sense for them meant the restoration of something which was important in their lives. It reminded them of home." He organised several services each Sunday and during the week the little church was used for discussion groups on all sorts of topics. "One would have imagined that enough religion was emanating from St George's throughout the day," he said, but there was a further request to put on a "quite short and simple" service at the end of each day.

"Each evening then, at nine o'clock the Church is dimly lit with the Altar candles, and a small floodlight on the Altar Cross [the floodlight had been cobbled together from a car's headlamps], and the Church is packed with dim crouching or kneeling forms. It is not a service; we say our own prayers and are occupied with our own thoughts for ten minutes. It is rather wonderful, nothing is planned nor spectacular, merely the real need of the men fulfilled in an atmosphere of quietness which is what they had lacked and desired."

During the week the little church was used for discussion groups on all sorts of topics.
Pencil drawing by POW Mike Hardy 3rd June 1942

If my father had felt any qualms about using an abandoned mosque for Christian worship he was soon put at ease by an unexpected visitor.

"On a wet afternoon a little bearded Indian arrived on the pillion of a motorcycle. He came straight to me where I was busy giving a talk in Church. He introduced himself as the Moslem priest whose mosque we were now using. He had come for his prayer books which, fortunately, I had saved and kept hidden in my cupboard. He was overjoyed to receive them and in 'pidgin' English we introduced each other as 'padres' of religion. He rather surprised me with his broadminded remark that he was glad that I was using his building, and that it was being used for the worship of God."

St George's Mark 1: the mosque was converted into a church with new furnishings lovingly made by the prisoners. *Watercolour painting by Lieut.Eric Stacy R.E. 1943*

The Moslem priest whose mosque Eric was using surprised him with his broadminded remark that he was glad that they were using his building and that it was being used for the worship of God.
Drawing by POW C B Lee March 1942

Gradually St George's was refurbished. The nave was carpeted with coconut matting, and the men in the workshops made altar rails and a pulpit and even reconditioned a wheezy old harmonium. My father also made his own communion wine with raisins, water and sugar, and wisely did not question where these supplies had come from. "I wish it were possible to convey the thrill which I get each day in wandering through the various workshops and seeing the progress that has been made and in delighting in the skill and workmanship that has gone into that progress. Seats for latrines, new handles for shovels are necessary jobs but how much more exciting it is to build to a given plan and design something which will make the Church more beautiful." How much more dedicated too when the workmen had few tools to use: "They have a few badly worn hacksaw blades, and after much hammering and forging, it may take a day to file a groove the thickness of a finger."

The weeks began to stretch into months. A university was created and my father was put in charge of the Theological Faculty which had 30 students. Life settled into a quietly productive routine and the men used their professional skills to create rice-milling machines and to build showers and they kept their spirits up by putting on top class plays and concerts.

But right from the early days of imprisonment the men were on starvation rations of rice which they did their best to supplement with any kind of vegetables or scraps of meat or dried fish they could get hold of, but soon they were suffering from diseases brought on by lack of vitamins. "We are starving, not melodramatically, but slowly," he wrote. Often he officiated at 5 or 6 funerals a week. "The grim thought comes into one's mind that many of these crosses cover the mortal remains of men reported safe after battle. Men who need not have died but for the facts and conditions of our captivity".

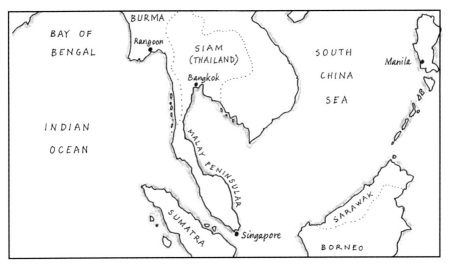

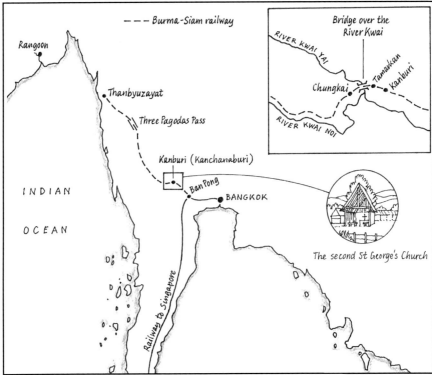

Maps of the Malay Peninsular in the 1940s. The POWs travelled from Singapore to the
staging post at Ban Pong (Bampong) in iron trucks, a journey which lasted 5 days.
The track of the Burma-Siam Railway on which they laboured is shown with a dotted line.
Kanburi (Kanchanaburi) staging camp and Kanburi Hospital, where Eric Cordingly was
based, were situated close to the River Kwai. *Drawn by David Cordingly*

The routine of this life of imprisonment continued for many months but gradually their numbers were depleted. The Imperial Japanese Army decided to make use of the labour at their disposal and prisoners were being sent off in working parties, and sinister news filtered back about those who were being sent to work "up-country". They were to be used as slave labour on the infamous Thai-Burma Railway which was being built to secure the Japanese supply lines inland from Tokyo to Burma. The prisoners were set to work on an almost impossible task of construction: 258 miles through mountains and thick jungle to be completed in 18 months.

When it was my father's turn to go with his force, "F" Force, not knowing what horrors awaited ahead, he carefully packed up the portable church furnishings, taking special care of the brass cross, and he saw everything safely loaded on to lorries for the train journey.

Just after midnight on Easter Day 1943 he was transported up-country, as all the others had been, crammed 28-30 men to a wagon in iron cattle trucks which, in the tropical heat, were baking like ovens. For 5 days and nights they rattled their way up to Thailand and when they finally arrived at the staging post at Bam Pong they were told they had a 160 mile trek ahead, marching overnight through the jungle: "I wonder if you realise how hopeless we felt," he wrote. At this point they had to abandon most of their belongings in order to march through the jungle, and the cross and the other precious church items he reluctantly left at a staging post in Bam Pong.

After 2 days marching my father was forced by illness to stop in Kanchanburi, close to the River Kwai, but once he was on his feet again he began his ministry to the men around him who were dying from the enforced slave labour on the death railway. He was appalled at what he saw.

"In months these men have lived in dense jungle with no shelter during the rains, their food has been plain rice, often as little as 3 spoonfuls 3 times a day, flavoured with onion and bean water. Men would be turned out before dawn, given a portion of rice and marched perhaps a mile or two to the railway. Here cuttings and embankments were being made. Bridges built, routes blasted through rock forms. Work would cease with the coming of darkness and they would be marched back to camp. Rain continued for days at a time. Men collapsed with malaria, dysentery, tropical ulcers, huge open wounds as large as a plate, many amputations followed these ulcers. Side by side with the prisoners worked conscripted coolie labour and (from them) soon swept through an epidemic of cholera, decimating our forces.

"Men would be turned out before dawn, given a portion of rice and marched perhaps a mile or two to the railway. Here cuttings and embankments were being made".
Painting by POW Des Bettany

Around 16,000 allied prisoners-of-war died during the construction of the
Thai-Burma Railway. *Painting by POW Des Bettany*

"The men were worn out by work which had kept them slaving during the hours of daylight, in almost continuous rain, barefooted because boots had fallen to pieces during the march, with no clothes except a ragged pair of shorts or some sort of rag for a loin cloth. Men were stunned and apathetic, but slowly the spiritual side revived and flourished as never before. Men had been so near death – life for them had been stripped of its veneer, stark reality had faced them, and they expected to be met on those terms. They talked about death and many is the time at the bedside of a dying man he has asked me to pray for his death, for his peace, for release from his abject misery."

"Many is the time at the bedside of a dying man he has asked me to pray for his death,
for his peace, for release from his abject misery."
Painting by POW Eric Stacy

These pencilled notes I discovered amongst the POW papers and artwork which my mother had tucked away for safe-keeping. Some of them are smudged and almost illegible, and they are written on scraps of airmail paper and a Thai child's exercise book and no doubt carefully concealed from the guards.

"It is too harrowing to picture vividly a ward of men whose sole kit consists of a tin and a spoon and a haversack and a piece of rag, lying on bare bamboo, or rice sacks with no covering, until later blankets were issued. The patients present a sorry picture, their exhaustion is so complete that no pain is suffered, they slip into a coma and the end is peaceful. Each morning several bodies are lying still."

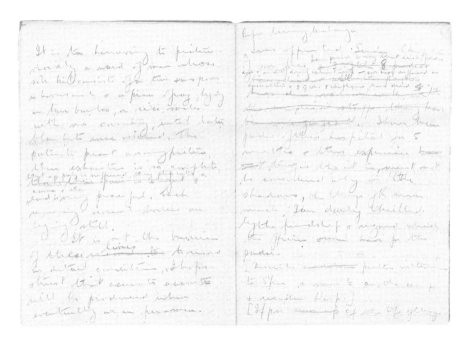

A page from Eric's notes, written hastily and in secret into a Thai child's exercise book. "It is too harrowing to picture vividly a ward of men whose sole kit consists of a tin and a spoon, a haversack and a piece of rag, lying on bare bamboo."

From April 1943 to April 1944 my father worked alongside the doctors in their makeshift hospitals near Kanchanaburi. He spent his time with the dangerously ill and dying men and then he took their burial services, sometimes several in a day. He also kept a neat Burial Register in which he recorded the details of the men who had died. Page after page containing their names, rank, religion, the causes of death and family details, so that he could write to their families if he got home. It is a heart-breaking document.

But he said that this experience, tragic though it was "it must not be considered only in the shadows, things of Christianity mean much. We built an open air Altar which I used for celebrations, whilst the evening services were informal and took place in the open shed [the 'hospitals' and sleeping quarters were no more than crude jungle huts].

Pencil sketch of St George's Mark II in Kanburi close to the River Kwai.
This "grand little chapel" was built entirely from odds and ends found round the camp.
It had bamboo uprights, grass mats and was roofed with tarpaulin.
Sketched by a POW 1.9 1943

"In describing the church built here [St Georges Mark 11] it compares poorly with the St George's of Changi – but still, a grand little chapel has been created, built entirely from odds and ends found in the camp and the only tool is a 4½" saw. The Chapel is built with bamboo uprights and grass mats form the sides and back, it is roofed with tarpaulin. The Altar is made from bamboo and mats with interlaced basket-like material as a reredos or background. Cross and candles are from bamboo as are the altar rails. Marmite jars are the flower vases – it is really quite an impressive little shrine and much admired by our Nip guards – and used well by us all."

Later he was able to rescue his church kit from the jungle staging post in Bam Pong. The bamboo cross was replaced by the precious brass cross and the altar was dressed once again with the furnishings used at St George's Mark 1 a year before.

When the Burma-Thailand Railway was completed at the cost, so it is said, of one man for every railway sleeper, the surviving men were sent back to Changi. First the fit and later the sick were moved from Thailand back to Singapore. My father and other chaplains volunteered to stay behind with the sickest men. Nearly two thirds of my father's force "F" force of 7000 men had perished, and of the 28 men with whom he had travelled in the railway truck, only 7 survived.

St George's Mark III June '44 – March '45 was constructed in No 2 Working Camp, which was situated immediately to the south and outside Changi Gaol building itself, but within Changi's prison walls. The brass cross can be seen on the altar in both these paintings.
Painting by POW Eric Stacy

St George's Mark IV April – September '45. St George's Mark III was moved
to the Officers' Area of Changi Prison. It was surrounded by their chicken runs
so it was affectionately known as St-George's-in-the-Poultry.
Painting by POW Eric Stacy

Back in Changi, for the next year, the men were no longer in the spacious Changi barracks area, but they were now crammed into the gaol itself and in huts they built around the prison walls. 12,000 POWs were crammed into an area intended for 800 civilian prisoners. Here, once again, my father organised volunteers to help him build an open air chapel which they called St George's Mark 111, with the polished brass cross gleaming on the makeshift altar again, until the IJA ordered them to move to a different area. In twenty four hours they moved the church from the old site to a new one beside the chicken runs, so St George's Mark 1V was affectionately known as St George's-in-the-Poultry. And there the cross remained. The war ended in Europe in May 1945, but still the POWs were held captive. Finally on August 15th, following the two bombs which were dropped on Hiroshima and Nagasaki, the Japanese signed their surrender. Three and a half years of imprisonment were at an end. The sick and starved men were released at last and put onto boats for the long journey home.

* * * *

Years later, my father's death prompted these vivid memories of Changi from fellow POW Dick de Grey:

"There stood among the barrack areas to which we were confined, a beautiful little Mosque built for the use of Indian troops of the pre-war garrison. We got a message through to them asking whether they were willing to let us use their Mosque for Christian worship. To their lasting honour and charity they said 'yes'. So was born St George's with Eric in charge.

"Even after more than 30 years my heart is warm when I remember it: the lovely pulpit and Sanctuary fittings, the brass cross and candlesticks, all made by men from heaven knows what scrap materials. And the thronged services with Eric as their dynamic central figure.

"Then Eric was sent up-country to the appalling camps and slavery of the notorious 'Death Railway'. I met him the day he got back to Changi. He had, as nearly as I can recall, a pair of shorts, a pair of clogs, a vest of sorts and firmly grasped his portable communion set.

"Then we set to and built another St George's, much cruder, mostly open to the skies, but as ever crowded with men right up to the entrance to the Sanctuary - you couldn't keep them away. Even in those days his affectionate nickname was 'The Bishop'."

(in the 18th Division Association magazine, August 1976)

Pencil drawing by POW Mike Hardy on which he has written
"Padre Cordingly accompanied by Padre Davidson entering
St George's Church for Evensong. Changi 30.6.42"

* * * *

My father quietly got on with the rest of his life with very little reference to those wartime years. But, seven years before he died, he reflected on his experiences in a book called 'Beyond Hatred' in which he contributed a chapter to a collection of real-life stories about forgiveness.

"It was the most wonderful time in my life, in spite of the grim and hungry times" he wrote. "For once, and for three and a half years, the thin veneer of civilization, or reticence, had been stripped from men. We were all down to bedrock. One saw people as they really were."

"Looking back to the really grim time in the jungle camp beside the Railway, the truly remarkable thing was the way the human spirit rose to magnificent heights. After months of sheer degradation, gradually the spirit to care for one another revived, incredible kindness and self-sacrifice was in evidence".

He also spoke about his experiences to Anglia TV at around the same time:

"I think the life was real there, it was more real there than life's ever been, ever since. In a sense we'd found a way of living which was, to us, tremendously important and we were shattered at the end, when parachutists came in to the camp, at the brutal way they dealt with our captors. We had learnt to live with them, we had got a way of life, we had got a faith, goodness mattered, caring for each other mattered and this was something which meant a very great deal to us."

* * * *

As I held the cross in my hands in my mother's cottage 18 years later, I finally appreciated the faithfulness of my father's ministry under such extreme conditions. And I understood that this modest brass cross had served as a beacon of light, hope and love during those long, dark years of imprisonment.

Before my brother John and I set off for Singapore I wanted to see if I could track down any of the ex-POWs who had known St George's and maybe I could even find the man who had made the cross. By chance ex-POW Jack Chaplin had already begun some research into the whereabouts of the church furnishings and had written to my mother, so I contacted him. He said he could not trace the man who had constructed the cross out of the brass shell case, but he gave me the address of the sapper who had done the engraving. He also arranged for me to meet a group of men in his house in Ipswich. This was getting exciting. I approached the BBC Radio 4 "Sunday" programme and was told they would be interested in a feature about the return of the cross (broadcast on BBC Radio 4 April 5th 1992).

Tim Hemmings of the 560th Royal Engineers. He was only 21 when he was asked to engrave the regimental badges on to the trefoils on the cross. He used an engraving tool he had made out of an old umbrella stem.

Tim Hemmings, who had engraved the cross with the regimental badges, was a stonemason now living in Virginia Water in Surrey. I wrapped the cross up and took it to him, and as he unfolded the plastic bubble wrap he look astonished:

'Well I'm blowed, yes that's it! Who would've thought I'd see this again? Was it fifty years? Amazing. Hasn't it kept well?"

"Do you remember doing the engraving on it?" I asked

"Yes I do, and you know it's amazing, I couldn't visualise whether the badges were cut deep enough to withstand all this time and cleaning but there it be. The base was made from a 4.5 howitzer shell and of course I had no tools or anything but I found an old umbrella stem. The centrepiece was quite good steel so I made a couple of engraving tools out of that. I was quite a blacksmith and I used to make tools. I buried them all in the bottom of the hut [when he went up country], I expect they are still there! I was happy as anything to do these jobs and, well I suppose it took your mind off it, that was the thing. You kept on going and if you gave in you could die standing up as it were. A lot of our chaps died like that. They just gave up and that was the end of it."

"Why do you think you were chosen to do the engraving?"

"I was the only one that could do it. I was 21. They kept me busy engraving things. It was helpful to be busy. Most of the time you were out working digging ditches or roads. I had a very good training as a stonemason and carver and I worked with some wonderful old craftsmen. And it just rubbed off. I enjoyed it. We had a game making these things – things were so damn scarce it was a difficult job to make anything like that. Cutting one of those shell cases in half was quite a job because it was thick metal."

"How did you fix the trefoils to the cross?"

"They produced this silver solder [in the workshop], and that's what we put the trefoils on with. We had a big copper soldering iron so that you could hot it up and use it for soldering work and we used to have a coke fire."

Tim was one of the first of the POWs to be sent to work on the railway and he remained there until it was completed. In the beginning he worked with explosives. "We used to do a lot of demolition work: chimneys and things that the aircraft could home in on and knew where they were. I had a good name for being an explosives expert," he said. Then he became one of the "spikers" who used to drive the nails into the wooden sleepers: "Nothing very professional but it worked. The trouble was you didn't get enough food and of course the Koreans were the worst people to deal with. The Japs didn't like the Koreans and the Koreans passed it down the ladder on to us. It was nothing to make you stand holding a rock over your head facing the sun and they'd keep turning you round so you faced the sun and eventually you just collapsed in a heap."

"Did that happen to you?"

"Yes, it happened to anybody that caused a bit of a rumpus. Well it's a long time ago now isn't it?" Tim and his fellow POWs experimented with eating anything which might provide them with protein: snakes, lizards, bats, rats, any fish they could hook, but he said he drew the line at eating a monkey. "You just did your best to keep alive and that's as much as you could do. You just took things as they came along. 'Do unto others as you would wish them to do unto you' – that's me. I'm not particularly religious at all. But if you go on like that you're not doing bad. I've had an extraordinary life really."

IMPERIAL JAPANESE ARMY

Date 23·5·かかか

Your mails (and   ) are received with thanks.
My health is (good, usual, poor).
I am ill in hospital.
I am working for pay (I am paid monthly salary).
I am not working.
My best regards to MUM DAD THELMA,
AND ALL AT HOME.

Yours ever,

Jim,

The POWs were finally allowed to send a postcard home in May 1944.
Tim significantly included the name of the young woman, Thelma,
he had met at a dance three weeks before he left.

Tim and Thelma were married in London in 1947

Tim Hemmings had a good homecoming. The young woman he had met at a dance three weeks before he left to go to war, was waiting on the station platform for him when he got back. Thelma was a WAAF during the war and survived several bombing raids on London. He also returned to the same stonemason's firm and worked there until he was 70. He spent some time restoring numerous monuments around the country, including the Kennedy Memorial at Runneymede, and the frieze of angels on the exterior wall of Canterbury cathedral. But he never forgot the engraving he had done on the cross and was astonished at how many lives it had touched: "I never thought when we made this cross up it would travel around like this."

Then I took it to the group of ex POWs in Suffolk, and their memories too came flooding back as they took the cross in their hands: "I can remember the altar as it was with the cross and the candlesticks" said Jack Chaplin, "It was a peaceful area. It was sort of set apart to some extent". Len Barber agreed: "With all the work that was done by the POWs they turned it into what we'd call a nice small English church. They had services at the church morning, afternoon and evening because there were so many prisoners roaming around and, in fact, there were times when people were standing waiting to come to the next service before the other service had really finished you know".

"You used to wander up to the church and round that area when you had a chance" remembered Harry Rolfe, "For that was sort of a quiet place really and you didn't know what was happening, and I mean you sort of lived from day to day and I didn't say my prayers very often but most often at night you had a thought and you said a quiet prayer to yourself very often: when are you going to get out of this muddle?"

A POW entering the converted mosque in the early morning.
The prisoner is carrying his mess tin and cup which he will use for breakfast later.

Treasuring all these vivid memories I wrapped the cross up again and returned home and tucked it into my suitcase and my mother wrote a letter for us to take to the Changi Museum:

"The return of the altar cross to St George's, Changi, is, I believe, where my husband would wish it to be. Many of the survivors of those prisoner of war days and, in the future, their families, will visit Singapore and catch a glimpse of what, by now, fifty years later, is part of history. He once told me that he was able to be of more use as a priest in those terrible years, than at any time in his life. Though he buried many friends there he also made many friends for life. We are happy, as a family, to hand over the cross to you on permanent loan."

My brother and I set off for Singapore in February 1992, and we arranged to meet the Reverend Henry Khoo who was Changi Prison Chaplain, like his father and grandfather before him. The museum at that time was just outside the looming grey walls of Changi Gaol, which still operates as a civilian gaol, and we were given a tour of the building by the prison governor. The prisoners jumped to attention as we walked past their rooms: "Morning Sir!" It was an uncomfortable experience and I was very relieved to get outside and wander around the little, reconstructed, open air chapel. It was bordered with large flowering bushes of frangipani, their exotic white blooms filling the air with their sweet fragrance, and the altar of the chapel was covered with red and yellow hibiscus flowers and notes from visiting relatives.

Reverend Khoo greeted us warmly and conducted a moving little service in the open air chapel as we handed over the cross."I believe that we're going to put that cross right at this particular chapel," he told us, "As we'll most likely describe to the visitors how the cross came to be made and the significance of it and I believe it's going to bring back memories. Pleasant ones and memories of how God was to them during the time of their suffering and incarceration". He gave a special blessing as he held the cross in his hands:

On March 18th 1992 Reverend Henry Khoo conducted a short service in
Changi Chapel for the handover of the brass altar cross. It was presented by Dr John
Cordingly and his sister Louise, on behalf of their mother Mary Cordingly.

"We thank you that this cross, once a symbol of shame, has become
a symbol of hope for each one of us here, as well as for those that were
interned here."

And then he placed the cross once again on the altar of a chapel in
Changi in Singapore. By now this cross had travelled over 16,000 miles.

After the service one of the visitors came up to us with tears in
her eyes:

"It looks just what a chapel in those days would've looked like you
know, because it's built with local materials and then inside there
are lots of small messages from people who've visited and it's quite
moving really.

I've witnessed the war in London with the bombings and that you know. It takes you back and, yes, you think of the young fellows dying. The way they died which was tragic. I think it's terrific and I think they should always keep it as a memorial."

The cross was placed on the altar of Changi Chapel amongst the hibiscus blooms and notes left by visitors to the chapel.

* * * *

With the cross back in Changi, this could have been the end of the story, but it wasn't.

I joined an organisation in the UK called Children of Far East Prisoners of War (COFEPOW) which has a lively, quarterly newsletter, always including the names of new members and their relationship to a POW. Out of the blue a card dropped on to my doormat in London.

"I remember Padre Cordingly very well. I thought about him all these years wondering what happened to him when we were freed. I used to help him prepare the services in Changi Jail. I liked your dad very much; he helped me and others to have hope and faith."

I called the telephone number on the card and spoke to Bertie Boyce, now in his 90s, who had been a butcher's delivery boy in Dereham in Norfolk when he was called up.

"I remember St George's Church and was found in there at every chance I had. Each night I would make tracks to sit in silent prayer and sometimes have a chat to a chaplain. Here was when I got to know your dear father who provided comfort to me because I was not feeling worth much and left in the far part of the world with no chance of seeing my family again. I was attending daily funerals and thinking: who's next, is it me? But through prayers and the services and your dad's sermons I rebuilt my life and felt a trust all would be fine.

"My grandmother back home in Dereham, Norfolk, unbeknown to me also prayed for my safe return. I found her ill in bed when I did get home. She told me she prayed to live to see me come home and she was so happy to know I also prayed to come home to see her again. She lived to see me marry Wyn the girl next door".

Bertie Boyce married Wyn, "the girl next door" in Dereham in 1946.

Bertie and I kept up a correspondence until his death in 2014, and he poured his thoughts into his letters: "There were many FEPOWs could never show any forgiveness and it was always like a canker tormenting them. I am able to say that I never felt that way but all the same I did not forget - not in a hateful, revengeful way but for me it has always been about my school pals who joined up with me just before the outbreak of the war and most never came home. It was difficult for me to face the mothers of my schoolboy friends, some even asked me "Why have you come home when my boy has not?" It took a long time to heal that wound so to speak. I found moving away soon after we married gave me a good start in a fresh place where I was unknown."

Bertie told me that when he first got home he relished his freedom so much he used to spend hours cycling round the neighbourhood in Dereham and he used to sit in the fields and pat the grass and say to himself "This is my country". He became the caretaker of a stately home in Yorkshire, and also a volunteer prison chaplain. He said he thought he could be helpful as a prison visitor because he understood what it felt like to be imprisoned.

Bertie and Wyn Boyce in Yorkshire in 2012. Later in life Bertie worked as a volunteer prison chaplain because he said he understood what it felt like to be imprisoned.

* * * *

Meanwhile in Pontypridd in South Wales, Bernard Stogden had begun his own research into his father's prisoner of war years in the Far East. Tragically for Bernard, his father did not return home. He died on 17th September 1945, aged 38, one month after the war ended. Bernard and his two sisters were born before the war. Bernard was 4, his sister Beryl was 2 and baby Freda was less than a year old when their father set sail. And theirs was a double tragedy because their mother died of pneumonia at the age of 24 a year after he left. The orphans were separated. Bernard and Beryl were brought up by their maternal grandmother and Freda was sent to live with her father's sister so they were never a family again. Bernard's grandmother was, herself, a World War 1 widow.

Harry Stogden aged 28.

"The different governments that have the power have never thought - what about the children of these brave men? We don't get a look in, neither do we ever get a mention. We just have to get on with it," said Bernard. "I felt that we were discarded. My father gave his life so that we that are left could go free and yet there was no reparation for us. From the human point of view – and by today's standards, everything seemed very gloomy. I am very sorry we were not told of my father's younger life or his war record. As Beryl and myself were often at the same school together, we were almost felt to be left out being war orphans and no one seemed concerned. Apart from my dear Grandmother who died when I was 15. You see we were brought up with my grandmother and step-grandfather and I used to call my grandmother 'Nanny' and my step-grandfather 'Dad'. He took the place of my father. But he wasn't my father. He was very, very strict. But he brought us up and I have no complaints about that."

Bernard had only the bare bones of information about his father's short life and death. Harry was born at Finchley Park, one of five children, and his father was a professor of music and his mother an accomplished pianist. He met and married Phyllis, a Welsh girl up from Pontypridd who had come to work in North London where he lived in Edmonton. Phyllis was 18 and Harry was 28. He was a mechanical engineer and worked for the Advanced Laundry in Noel Street London W1 where he was highly thought of.

Phyllis aged 18

Like my father, Harry was imprisoned in Changi prison camp for over a year (until May 1943) where his skills as a mechanical engineer were put to good use in the prisoners' workshops, although, like many other POWs, he was in and out of Roberts Hospital in Changi, with dysentery and other illnesses brought on by their starvation diet. He was then sent in a working party to Japan and ended doing hard labour in the coal mines in Fukuoka.

This is the last photograph of Harry Stogden. It was taken at Fukuoka POW camp after liberation by the Americans. Harry, looking very gaunt, is second row back, third from the left wearing a cap. He also has the swollen stomach of someone suffering from beri beri.

Work in the coal mines was notoriously difficult and dangerous and in some places the conditions were as bad as those on the Thai-Burma Railway. However, Harry survived until the war ended and then he was taken by the Americans who arrived to liberate their camp and he was put on to the hospital ship the USS Haven at Nagasaki. He died suddenly on board the USS Haven from beri-beri [a nutritional disorder resulting from lack of Vitamin B]. Bernard contacted the sail maker and seaman who had fetched Harry's body and stitched it into the canvas shroud for burial. He told Bernard that he "didn't look too bad." He said: "Harry was coming along alright but all of a sudden he died." His body was then transferred to the British aircraft carrier HMS Speaker and he was buried with full military honours at sea in the waters just off Nagasaki.

Harry Stogden's body was transferred to British aircraft carrier HMS Speaker and buried with full military honours in the waters off Nagasaki.

Harry's son Bernard met the bugler in this photograph at a ship's reunion.
The bugler was a member of the Salvation Army and he told Bernard that
the crew were all very moved by Harry's burial service at sea.

In 1997 Bernard was in his fifties, and like many other FEPOW
children at this age, he began his research into his father's war years.
Bernard, like his father, is skilled with his hands and he founded and ran
a successful joinery business in Pontypridd. One morning in the autumn
of 1997 he read some information which hit him like a thunderbolt.

"I found out about my Dad and the Cross by pure accident. I became a member of the Japanese Labour Camp Survivors Association and we used to get these newsletters, called "The Fulcrum" every so often. I can remember we'd been out shopping on Saturday and came home and Edith, my wife, said: 'This letter came for you today' and I knew what it was. It was a letter from this organisation and there was a front page story about the St George's Cross, Changi, of how it was made by a Staff Sergeant in the RAOC, the only name that they had was his Christian name 'Harry'. The words were jumping out of the page. I knew this man must be my father. I was so excited that I decided to ring the telephone number under this article and on telephoning Mr Bill Holtham (an ex POW himself) who wrote the story, I introduced myself that I believed that this soldier was my father.

"Yes it is – it is!" he said. "I'm ever so pleased that you rang" and he gave me all the information about what my father had done. I couldn't put the phone down. I had tears in my eyes when he was telling me. We had quite an emotional chat. He told me of how he couldn't remember the surname as he always called him Staff, but he was also his friend. He told me he used to watch the progress of making the cross, of how my father used to come back to the hut of an evening and show how he had progressed in the making of it.

FULCRUM

Issue No.. 54   Winter 1997

THE ST. GEORGE'S CROSS. CHANGI

Known by many ex-Far East prisoners as "The Changi Cross", shown opposite, it came into being shortly after the fall of Singapore. Under the guidance of Capt. Akester, of the 18th Division Ordnance Workshops, and with the help of the experts, an engineering workshop was built up from material scrounged from the surrounding area.

The cross itself was made by a Staff Sergeant of the R.A.O.C. unfortunately only his first name, 'Harry', is remembered. The base of the cross was fashioned from the base of a 4.5 howitzer shell, the rest from carefully fashioned strips of brass. At each of the four ends it carried trefoils engraved with facsimiles of the cap badges of 'Royal Army Ordnance Corps', 'Royal Engineers', 'Royal Northumberland Fusiliers' and the 'Royal Army Service Corps'. The base was engraved with the badge of the 'Royal Artillery'. At a later date an unknown person added the wording 'St. George's Church and 'Prisoner of War Camp 1942-1945 to the base. These engravings were done by Tim Herrings, Royal Engineers.

The conversion of the mosque, the first home of the Cross, in what had been India Lines, was carried out by Edward Wincott R.E.s, who started the pulpit and alter rails. The plaque of St. George and the Dragon was made by Robert Payne and Harry Ralph, also R.Es. A Pair of candlesticks were lovingly looked after by Cpl. Sid Roper, R.A.O.C., who brought them home and they are now in the Imperial War Museum.

The church was closed when "F" Force was sent up country. Padre Cordingly took with him the alter cross and the plaque of St. George to Bampong along with other ornaments. I picked up with the Bishop (as he was affectionately known) in 'Kamburi' where he re-established St. George's Church (Mark 111). Eventually the Cross and plaque were brought home by Padre Cordingly then in 1992 on Mrs Cordingly's suggestion the cross was returned to Singapore where it was handed over to the Rev. Henry Khoo at the Memorial Chapel. On permanent loan from the Cordingly family the Cross has been mounted in a Perspex fronted box and fixed to the rear of the alter. There is no doubt it adds a great deal to the feeling within the Memorial Chapel in Changi, a virtual replica of the original.

In all humility, The Cross will continue to remind us of all who helped others, those unfortunate and wonderful comrades who did not return home, and those who, after their return, suffered and untimely death. I would particularly like to thank Jack Capiin, for his devotion in tracing the cross, and the other artefacts. Including Sid Roper, and all the lads who made this account possible.

This story, and the photograph of the cross, were provided by Bill Holtham.

In 1997 a front page story about the St George's Cross appeared in The Fulcrum, the newsletter of the Japanese Labour Camp Survivors Association.

"He told me how my father used to make sewing needles for the machines that they had managed to scrounge and how he had made artificial limbs for the men. Believe me I couldn't have felt more proud to listen to all the marvellous things that my Dad had done".

Bernard alerted The Western Mail and an article appeared in it a week later. Bill Holtham was quoted again:

"When we arrived at Changi we had to wire ourselves into the camp, build the camp ourselves. We sent out 'scrounger' parties to collect whatever we could find and we could use. We set up a workshop with all the materials we had or could scrounge. I watched every step of the cross being produced. The base of the cross was made from half a howitzer artillery shell, the rest from carefully fashioned strips of brass".

A 4.5" howitzer brass shell case dated 1918, made by Curran Metal and Munitions Company in Cardiff. It came from a collection near Ypres, Belgium and it was used on the Western Front during World War 1. It is similar to the one used to make the base of the Changi Cross.

Harry Stogden. Harry used his extraordinary gifts as an engineer to make self-locking joints for artificial limbs and new needles for sewing machines and also to make electrical repairs to vehicles in the camp. He spent some time fashioning the cross out of the howitzer shell case and other strips of brass in the prison workshops.

"I knew Harry very well", he said. "We were both in the Ordnance Corps. I can see him now, tall, curly hair, coming into the hut to show us the progress he had made on the cross. He was an extraordinary man. He was a very clever engineer. He designed a self-locking joint to use in artificial limbs we made for soldiers who had lost limbs. He made new needles for the sewing machines we used to repair our uniforms. He was a quiet, gentle man. He was a friend."

Bernard was now anxious to find all the information he could about his father. He taught himself to use the computer so that he could widen his research online. Then he contacted his sister Beryl who reminded him that she had recently found their father's blue American Red Cross bag in her attic when she moved house. He said that opening the bag of his father's belongings was "like looking into an Aladdin's Cave".

He found a notebook with Harry's name on the cover and looking inside he saw that his father had neatly written some notes in the form of an affectionate letter to his wife, not knowing, of course, that she had died. It was about 18 pages long and full of news about his situation and plans for their family's future together when he returned home. The first entry was dated one day after their surrender.

The cover of Harry's journal, written in the form of a letter to his wife Phyllis.

The first page of Harry's letter to Phyllis. He kept the journal from January to May 1943 while he was imprisoned in Changi before he was sent off to work in Japanese mines

EXTRACTS from Harry's letter to his wife

Changi Prisoner of War Camp, A letter to my beloved wife 16.1.43

"My darling Phyllis

Although I am not in a position to receive letters from you (I have not heard from you for 12 months) I have thought I would like to write to you".

After sailing 23,000 miles on the sea we were roped in as prisoners and we were marched to a place on this island called 'Changi' a distance of 15 miles. Here all of the prisoners were put, 45,000 of us. Gloom and despair was within all of us as you can imagine.

Our rations, small as they were lasted only a few days, soon they were gone.

The Japanese informed us that the only food they could give us was Rice, about 1 oz of meat per man per day and a few vegetables and that is all we have been living on.

Well the meat did not last very long, the ration of 'veg' has got smaller and smaller and now remains the rice. 'Bread', we forget what it looks like.

Prison life is far from nice, there is work to do of course but the Japanese are our masters although our own officers are with us. The food is very poor as you can imagine, diseases of all kinds break out everywhere, many men have died and most others are in a very bad state of health.

As for myself I have been comparatively lucky but I have been nearly blind for 6 months but thank God I am alright now. By the way, medical supplies like the food are getting very low, the matter is serious.

Well my dear, there is one thing to be said for prison life, it brings out the Best in a man, also the worst.

We have small churches here and I seem to have become a very interested member, C of E I am [Church of England]. I have learnt a lot about "Christianity", the life of Jesus Christ on this earth and his teachings.

Yes darling, I have changed a little for the better.

I do hope to be with you soon and I do want to love and care for my wife and our children as I have never done before. I always think of you in my prayers trusting that God will look after you all.

April 15th 43

Well dear, here I am again, have been in hospital [Roberts Hospital)] for a few weeks with a little stomach trouble but am getting along quite well now. I have been dreaming about you and the children for many nights now and I wonder sometimes if you dream of me. Sometimes they are nice dreams, sometimes not quite so nice. Many of the troops have been moved away up country, many more are going in a few days' time. I still remain behind; just where I shall finish up I don't know. How are things with you now, hope you are not worrying too much. You must excuse this writing as this is an awful pen and ink, still it is better than none, (I shall have to write single pages now as the ink goes right through).

Good Friday April 23rd 43.

Am still in the hospital, this is the 8th week, have had "Diarrhoea" but rid of that now but have got painful feet, all due to poor food. However we must trust good fortune. More troops are going away this week-end; don't know where they are going to.

Today is Easter Sunday 1943

To-day dear I think I will tell you my plans for the future. After my discharge the first thing I would like to do is to take you and the children for a holiday to somewhere, anyway there is a holiday for you and me. Well then the next thing is for me to find a job. …I would like to go away from London to the provincial districts, you know – near the country but not too far from the town, somewhere where houses are cheaper, also rents and the cost of living, but I would like to discuss this with you. ..I think there will be plenty of jobs in my line as there will be plenty of work after the war.

Well after that comes the question of finding a house, the most difficult job of all but never mind. When we have found one I have big ideas of Electricity.

If it is not laid on I would do it; I would like to go in for Electric cooking, heating, fires etc and be independent of coal, as it is so much cheaper and cleaner, perhaps we could keep chickens.

I want to make it my business to see that our children get the best education that we can give them. So you see I have quite a lot to talk to you about.

May 1st 1943

Another new month dear, doesn't the time fly. I am still in the hospital, am pretty well but under observation, am just as well off here as anywhere else so I am not worrying. A lot of mail has arrived in camp, am wondering if there is one for me, I hope so as it would cheer me up no end.

Nothing much has happened since my last entry, more troops are going away and things are generally quiet so will wind up for today.

Hallo dear, a few more lines for you, am out of the hospital now and am on a draft. Am going away soon but of course I don't know where.

Am feeling pretty well dear but am very weak, however I can get about and am all in one piece which is something to be thankful for. I hope you and the children are well dear". [Diary ends]

Changi Prisoner of War Camp, A letter to my beloved wife 16.1.43

"My darling Phyllis

Although I am not in a position to receive letters from you (I have not heard from you for 12 months) I have thought I would like to write to you".

He followed this greeting with a detailed account of their long journey by sea to Singapore Island. And then, every few days or weeks, he made another entry, sometimes talking about their starving conditions and his resulting ill health but always putting a brave face on things. Other entries speak longingly of his future together with his wife and family, and his plans to buy a house in the provinces and to make sure his children would have a good education.

He also spoke about the constant movement of working parties of troops away from Changi to unknown destinations in the service of 'their masters' the Japanese. The final entry in his notebook is dated May 1st 1943:

Hallo dear, a few more lines for you, am out of the hospital now and am on a draft. Am going away soon but of course I don't know where.

Am feeling pretty well dear but am very weak, however I can get about and am all in one piece which is something to be thankful for. I hope you and the children are well dear". (Diary ends)

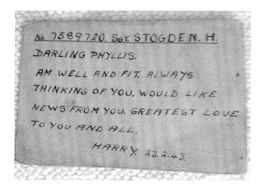

*Harry wrote this postcard to Phyllis not knowing
that she had died of pneumonia 4 months earlier*

Harry was then transported by sea to work in the Japanese mines. In the Red Cross bag Bernard also found a letter Phyllis's mother had written to the POW camp, informing Harry that his wife had died.

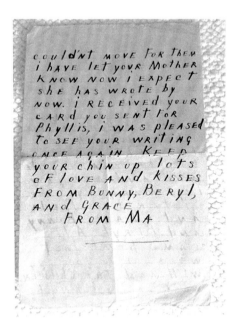

Harry's mother-in-law had to write this poignant letter to him.

1.8.1943

Dear Harry, I have wrote before to tell you about Phyllis. She passed away last October 14th 1942. I hope you will get this letter. The children are quite well and are growing. Margery your sister has Freda and I have Bunny and Beryl. Alf came home last week. He is looking well and the children were excited and he couldn't move for them. I have let your mother know now I expect she has wrote by now. I received your card you sent for Phyllis, I was pleased to see your writing once again. Keep your chin up.

Lots of love and kisses from Bunny, Beryl and Grace

from Ma

Bernard now had a vivid account of Harry's war years, and there was another vital link to make before he and Edith set out for Singapore to see the cross for the first time. At the end of the article in 'The Fulcrum' there was a reference he wanted to follow up:

"The church was closed when 'F' Force was sent up country. Padre Cordingly took with him the altar cross along with other ornaments. Eventually the Cross was brought home by Padre Cordingly."

Luckily for Bernard, "Cordingly" is an unusual name. But in 1997 it still took him weeks to discover my brother's name 'Dr John Cordingly' in the London telephone book and, rather startled, John put Bernard through to me. I was stunned to hear that we had finally discovered the name of the man who had made the cross. But Bernard was deeply disappointed to find that my father had died some 21 years earlier "I would have loved to have met him" he said, "I'd like to meet anyone who knew my father".

Two days later I received a letter from Bernard: "Since our chat last evening I read my father's notebook that I was telling you about and he does say in one part and I quote 'I seem to have become a very interested member of the church, C of E I am. I have learnt a lot about Christianity, the life of Jesus Christ on this earth and his teachings.' I believe my father must have had a lot of contact with your father especially if he was making the cross with your father's instructions. They must have had a lot in common with each other, don't you think so? They must have been good friends."

For 58-year-old Bernard, the visit to Changi Museum the following year (1998) was the culmination of a lifetime's loss and longings. "If I could travel to Singapore and see the cross, that would be as close to ending my search and my journey as possible. As close as I'll ever get."

In 1998 Bernard travelled to Singapore to see and to hold the cross which his father had made. "I took it out of the case and I held it. It was a wonderful day."

Bernard and his wife Edith in Changi Museum Chapel in 1998.

When he finally arrived there he found himself quite overcome with emotion.

"It was a very moving time for me. I had to wait before I could go down and see the cross because there was a party of Japanese schoolchildren going around and when I finally got down to the place I absolutely broke down and the people that were there dispersed while I was in this situation. And then I said "I'm alright now" and the Singapore lady I'd been in contact with, Rosalind Tan, said "This is your father's cross" and I said "Can I hold it?" and she said "Yes, we've unscrewed it all ready for you – just take the Perspex front off" and I took it out of the case and I held it. It was a wonderful day. I felt that my father had held it and he'd made it and that was a lot to me and I felt I was walking in his footsteps. Everywhere I went my father had been there. Wonderful. It was a very moving time."

Three years later the Old Changi Prison Chapel and Museum were closed to make way for the expansion of Changi Prison. On February 15th 2001 the Singapore Tourist board invited Bernard and his family to attend the opening of the new museum and chapel which had moved just 1km down the road. "I was guest of honour to place my father's cross on the altar" he said. "That again was very, very moving. I just couldn't keep my eyes dry at all. We sat there at the opening ceremony and Edith, my wife, nudged me and said "Look!" This young Singaporean man came and he had the cross in this wicker basket and asked me to put it on the altar, which I did. Seven of us went and we were treated like royalty. I will never forget it. It was just great to show my kids and their kids what a wonderful man my father must have been."

And there was one more surprise to come.

Bernard was aware of a roll of 80 photographic negatives in Harry's Red Cross bag but he had not thought much about them. Amazingly Harry must have managed to keep a camera with him during the war. The camera was now missing and several of the negatives were speckled with age. Mostly they showed unidentified military scenes apparently in the Far East. Bernard looked through them all again slowly this time, and he had a 'eureka' moment when he recognised the glint of a cross on an altar in several of the tiny negatives. He posted some of these photos on a FEPOW Community website, including one photograph which showed a figure in a white cassock bending towards the altar. Bernard had no idea who he was.

This mysterious photograph of a figure in a white cassock spurred Bernard on to examine some photographic negatives which had been sent home in his father's Red Cross bag.

In 2007 my husband, Paul, was transferring my BBC radio programme about the return of the cross, on to disc, and doing some background research at the same time. He saw the photograph of this mysterious figure on the FEPOW Community website. He had a

hunch it might be my father so he contacted Bernard to ask if he knew who it was. Bernard re-examined the negatives and said that there were two more photos of the same figure and this time his face was visible but he did not know who he was. A scan of the negatives proved inconclusive but by now Bernard was inspired by an even more personal motive. He had also found on one of the negatives the image of a young boy and on another negative the image of a woman with a child, and he suspected this might be himself and his mother and Beryl. He took the negatives to a local photographer to be developed and

Photograph of Bernard as a young boy which his father carried with him throughout his captivity.

indeed the boy was him and the other image was a photo of Phyllis and Beryl. Harry had taken these photos of his family just before he left England and had carried them with him throughout the war.

Bernard emailed the developed photos of the unknown figure in the cassock back to us. Paul said: "The copies were very small, the size of the negatives, but I enlarged them and suddenly found myself looking at the face of Eric Cordingly in his church in Changi".

Historic photographs taken by Harry Stogden of Eric Cordingly standing in St George's
Mark 1 in Changi with the new brass cross on the altar. Taken around April 1942.

Unique photograph of the exterior of St George's, the converted mosque,
taken by Harry Stogden around April 1942.

This was truly a historic discovery. Harry and my father must have decided to take photographs of the new altar cross they had designed and made together in the early years of their imprisonment. They are unique photographs of St George's, the beautiful converted mosque, with the cross on the altar, and they represent, now, a little piece of history gone forever under the tarmac of the modern day Singapore, Changi Airport.

I still marvel that the cross has taken me on such an unexpected and happy journey to uncover the mystery of my father's POW years. I am even more thrilled that it has led Bernard to finding a close connection with the father he never knew. And perhaps he and I have also caught a glimpse of the extraordinary fellowship and love they all shared, during those dark war years.

"When you mentioned (last evening) about putting it all in a book" Bernard told me, "I honestly think that it is not just my story but it's a story about two men, two fathers that went about and made the St George's Cross together and that it was that cross that gave so many hope that one day it would all be over and that they would return to their families. Unfortunately mine never made it, but I'm glad that yours did.

"It seems that your father and mine still have a very big hand in this wonderful story. It's like as if they are looking down on us from above, having a big smile together. It's a friendship put together in heaven and they are certainly not forgotten along with all the other poor souls who perished."

Bernard and Louise sorting out their fathers' papers together.

Pontypridd Summer 2014.

APPENDIX

Two POW artists whose paintings are featured in this book:

Des Bettany at work in Australia

DES BETTANY

Des was born in Burnley in Lancashire in 1919, and trained as an analytical chemist. He worked in the chemistry lab of an artificial silk factory. But in 1940, like Harry Stogden and Eric Cordingly, he was evacuated from Dunkirk then sent out to the Far East.

When he was first imprisoned in Changi he worked on repairing the war damage in Singapore and the dock area and he later joined the working parties clearing the swamp land to build the Singapore Changi Airport.

But he had an unusual artistic gift and he used it to keep up the spirits of fellow POWs. He carried a sketchbook with him and drew a series of jokey, satirical cartoons about prison camp life, and caricatures of their prison guards as well as documentary sketches and colourful programmes for the theatre productions put on by the POWs. "Paints were manufactured from coloured earth from various depths, sometimes as deep as 12 metres" he said. "Colours ranged from white, ocre and brown to Indian red. These were dried, ground with bottles and mixed with rice water, and worked very well."

After the war he returned to England and studied art in Leeds. He married in 1946 and then in 1958, with his wife and three children, he moved to Australia, where he took up a teaching post in Whyalla and then eventually became Acting Principal of the South Australian School of Art in Adelaide.

He rarely spoke of his experiences but in 1991 he was persuaded by the Singapore Tourist Promotion Board to write down a few of his thoughts:

"What remains clear is that throughout the period of privation, starvation and slavery, hope faith and confidence in our eventual release remained optimistically constant.

"My personal worst moments came when I had to appear before the Japanese Commandant and an assortment of interpreters to try and explain away, to humourless Japanese Officers a book of political cartoons I had drawn. I had lent the book to a careless person who allowed it to fall into the hands of Japanese guards. This was at a time when the war was going badly for Germany and Japan and this was reflected in the cartoons. I was extremely lucky to get away with a whole skin."

He died in Adelaide, Australia in 2000 aged 81.

Since then his family have appreciated the return of some of his artwork, (scanned & emailed back), because Des gave so many sketches away to fellow prisoners. You can see more of his work on: www.changipowart.com

Coastal gun, Changi Singapore.
Painting by Des Bettany

Self-portrait of Eric Stacy painted in
Changi POW camp

ERIC STACY

Eric Stacy trained as a chartered architect. He was 30 when the war broke out and he became a Lieutenant in the Royal Engineers supervising the construction of pillboxes. He was sent to Singapore just two weeks before it fell.

When he was a POW in Changi he helped the Chaplains to design and construct much of the building and furnishing of the temporary churches. He was then in one of the parties sent up to complete the building of the Burma Railway at the beginning of the rainy season and he spent 8 months in the jungle. The conditions were so appalling that only 50% of his force survived.

After the war he moved to the Acoustics section of the Building Research Station in the UK and supervised projects including the sound insulation of schools under the flight path of Heathrow airport and improving the acoustics of the Albert Hall.

He married and had two children and turned from painting to woodcarving in his spare time. He was also very involved in his local church and contributed both professional architectural advice and woodcarvings for the building. He rarely talked about his experiences as a prisoner, but when his grandchildren asked him to write down some memories for a school project he told them this story:

"One day in August 1945 we were told Japan had capitulated and we were free. We all stayed up late discussing the wonderful news, but when at last I went to bed I could not sleep because of a stomach pain which had come on quite suddenly. The next morning I joined the sick-parade queue, waiting in the hot sun for an hour to see the medical officer.

He whisked me off at once to the operating theatre in our improvised hospital, having diagnosed acute appendicitis. That same day, within two hours of my 'coming to' after the operation, a medical orderly offered me a meat pasty, part of a first consignment from the Red Cross. It was the first meat I had tasted for nearly two years. Scrumptious! The doctor was horrified when I told him I had been given such solid fare so soon, but I thrived on it. I was soon on my feet and enjoying the new freedom to come and go as we pleased. The badly sick were soon flown out to better-equipped hospitals, but the moderately fit had to wait 4 or 5 weeks for ships to be assembled to take us home. In the meantime we could go for a stroll or a swim or perhaps visit a warship in Singapore harbour. It was on board a British battleship that I had my first hot bath for 3 and 1/2 years!"

He died in 2004 aged 95.

St George's Mark 1, the converted mosque.
Watercolour painting by Lieut Eric Stacy RE 1943

ACKNOWLEDGEMENTS

Firstly I want to thank Bernard Stogden for his kindness and generosity in allowing me to tell his father, Harry's story. And also for Edith and Bernards' patience and hospitality on our many visits to Pontypridd.

I could not have completed the project without the help of my three co-editors: Paul, James and Alice Reynolds: thank you for all your advice and your encouragement. My three brothers have given me priceless practical support throughout the project: David inspired my mother to send the cross back to Singapore and he also drew the maps, John and I travelled to Changi, Singapore for the handover of the cross, and Christopher's card publishing company, Art Angels, has published this book. (note: I have written the book under my maiden name 'Cordingly' in order to keep consistency with the previous book Down to Bedrock by Eric Cordingly, which I edited under the same name).

Special thanks to Wyn Boyce for allowing me to reproduce extracts from her husband, Bertie's letters which brought the years in Changi so vividly to life for me.

I'm very grateful to the Hemmings family for tracking me down and inviting me to meet up once again with Tim Hemmings, now 95. It was an extraordinary and timely coincidence.

Mr Terry Waite CBE has not only written a very moving introduction, but he also sent kind words of encouragement which have meant a great deal to me.

Huge thanks to Jeya Ayadurai, Director of Changi Museum, for his welcoming Foreword, and his generous support for this project. And also to Jon Cooper at Changi Museum for his invaluable practical help and excellent advice from afar.

Special thanks to Claire Berkeley who cast a professional eye over the typescript and offered valuable ideas. To Sue Wilson for saying that it was a story that had to be told, also, to all my dear supportive friends who have kept me going.

Des Bettany's family have given me permission to use his wonderfully atmospheric paintings, more of which can be seen on the website: www.changipowart.com

Eric Stacy's family contacted me following the publication of Down to Bedrock. I now have a chance to thank them for the use of several of their father's beautiful drawings, paintings and Christmas cards, many of which have been reproduced again in this book.

I have also included some original illustrations made by FEPOWs whose families we have been unable to trace. We are indebted to them for their work.

Photograph taken in Changi Chapel in 1992. Source: The Straits Times, copyright Singapore Press Holdings Limited. Reproduced with permission.

Permission has also kindly been granted by Changi Museum and Chapel for use of their photograph of The Changi Cross.

And The Lutterworth Press for use of extracts from Beyond Hatred, edited by Guthrie Moir and published in 1969.

With huge thanks to Alice Cutting for her work on the book design and to Jon Bliss for the cover illustration and also to Katie Thomas, Liz Rayner and Peter Moore Fuller: all at MADE Agency Ltd.

Book websites:
www.thechangicross.co.uk
www.downtobedrock.co.uk